Killing SIN HABITS

Conquering Sin with Radical Faith

Stuart Scott

with Zondra Scott

Conquering Sin with Radical Faith
© 2013 by Stuart Scott and Zondra Scott

Published by Focus Publishing
All Rights Reserved

All Scripture is taken from The Holy Bible,
English Standard Version (ESV®)
Copyright © 2001 by Crossway Bibles,
A publishing ministry of Good News Bibles

and

The New American Standard Bible (NASB)
Copyright © by The Lockman Foundation
All Rights Reserved

Cover Design by Melanie Schmidt

ISBN: 978-1-936141-15-9

Printed in the United States of America

Focus Publishing
PO Box 665
Bemidji, MN 56619

Dedication

It has been such a blessing for me to write this book with my dear wife Zondra. God, in His infinite wisdom and goodness, brought us together to love Him, to love each other and serve His church. She is by far the most excellent friend that God has graced me with on this earthly pilgrimage. Over the years of experiencing both joys and sorrows, God has grown us together in a most mutually sanctifying way.

Working on this project together has blessed us not only in ministry ways but in a practical "living it out at home" way. Our desire is that we may continue to implement these biblical truths in our lives and relationships by His grace and for His glory until we meet our Savior face to face.

Stuart Scott

Preface

Many people do not bother to read the preface of a book. In this case we would like to offer some up-front encouragement and give you some suggestions for getting the most out of these chapters. Please take the time to read this one!

The majority of what you are about to read has been used in intense counseling situations. Writing this book has brought to mind several special individuals who were once enslaved to serious life-dominating sins. Now they walk in freedom, enjoying restored or new relationships and glorifying God with their lives. It has been a great blessing to have a front row seat in witnessing the sufficiency of God and His truths transform these dear people. Others have needed what is in this book to help them really change habits of selfishness, worry and other more common sins that affect their walk with God, their relationships, their joy and usefulness.

Our best advice is that you not read this book in an academic or accelerated way. If you will work through the material in a personal way, taking the time to put into practice its biblical principles, it will make all the difference in renewing your life. We must go to the One who created us and act on what He has given us concerning our relationship with Him and our change for lasting transformation from the inside out. Here are some suggestions:

- Pray before you read. Make confession if needed and ask for God's help.
- Read all the verses written out and in the parentheses and personally interact with them.

- Read a small portion at a time, pray about it and seek to apply each one to your life before moving on.
- Involve another sister or brother, discipler or counselor in this journey for prayer and accountability.
- Especially follow through on the practical applications in chapter nine.

We have prayed for you, for your real treasure to be Christ, for faith to trust that God can do something new, and for your freedom in Him!

Stuart and Zondra

Table of Contents

Chapter 1

Repeating Pattern of Sin: Just Like Clockwork But it Can Stop!

Be appalled, O heavens, at this; be shocked,
be utterly desolate, declares the LORD,
for my people have committed two evils: they
have forsaken me, the fountain of
living waters, and hewed out cisterns for
themselves, broken cisterns that can
hold no water. "Is Israel a slave? Is he a
home born servant? Why
then has he become a prey?"
Jeremiah 2:12-14

I will walk at liberty for I seek your precepts.
Psalm 119:45 (NASB)

Whether you are not sure you want to *kill* anything, or you're reluctant to hope again for real and lasting change, reading this book and taking it to heart will be life-changing! The first passage you read above expresses something you may have heard or know very well, and then something you may not yet realize. They are: (1) something is very wrong that must be changed for your good and God's glory, and (2) Jesus, the Fountain of Living Waters is what you are really looking for. A true grasp of this latter truth is your path to realizing the first one. Jesus is the answer for your own *broken cistern* which is a sinful substitute for true satisfaction, strength, or peace.

1

The second passage is the hope (surety) to which you can cling as you work through this book. If God is your creator (and He is), and the all-wise Shepherd of your soul (because He is your Savior), then both the motivation and the liberating answers for your pattern of sin will be found in the counsel of His Word (John 17:17; 2 Peter 1:1-4).

There is a great story in Acts 27 that is relevant to any present day struggle with recurring sin. The Apostle Paul describes his challenging trip by sea to Rome. The beginning of the journey sounds like a modern day, tranquil cruise, stopping at various ports of call, ship changes, and friendly receptions. At one point, however, the weather showed signs that continuing the voyage might prove dangerous. Paul admonished the Captain and crew to consider wintering in a safe harbor. Before they could find safety, a storm came up and they were scarcely able to get the ship under control. In Paul's own words, "Since we were being violently storm-tossed, they (the crew) began the next day to jettison the cargo. And on the third day they threw the ships tackle overboard with their own hands" (v.18, 19). They sailed for fourteen days in this storm before they saw an island of refuge. Even then, they had to cut the anchors loose in order to sail to safety.

Paul's experience demonstrates to us the importance of throwing off that which hinders us in a true pursuit of Christ that leads to spiritual growth. The writer of Hebrews admonishes us to "Throw off that which hinders and the sin that so easily entangles. And let us run with perseverance the race marked out for us" (Hebrews 12:1). And yet, if you have experienced many failures concerning a particular sin, you most likely sense you are caught in a wearisome, seemingly hopeless cycle—one which you cannot seem to throw off.

It is very important to know exactly what's involved in the repeating pattern of sin. It is a cycle of lust (desire and worship) that happens *just like clockwork*. It begins to take shape in the perfect set up, actively starts with the first thought of temptation, and usually ends in failure, guilt and grief until the next time the perfect set up and temptation are present again. We can picture this cycle and each element involved like this:

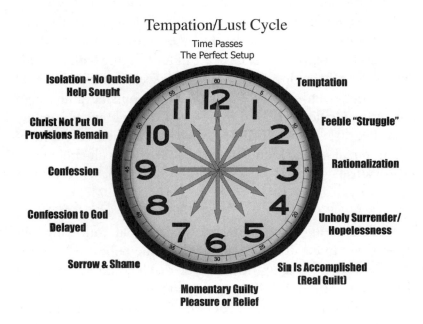

Temptation/Lust Cycle

Time Passes
The Perfect Setup

Isolation - No Outside Help Sought

Christ Not Put On Provisions Remain

Confession

Confession to God Delayed

Sorrow & Shame

Temptation

Feeble "Struggle"

Rationalization

Unholy Surrender/ Hopelessness

Sin Is Accomplished (Real Guilt)

Momentary Guilty Pleasure or Relief

But each person is tempted when he is lured and enticed by his own desire. Then desire when it has conceived gives birth to sin, and sin when it is fully grown brings forth death.
James 1: 14-15

As each segment (or state in which you find yourself) ticks away without interruption, it pushes forward to the next. Whether you are struggling with a lack of self-control with the television, the computer, gaming, food-related sin, sexual sin, drug abuse, spending money wrongly, the approval of others or some other sin or refuge, you will most likely see yourself in this progression.

1. Temptation: The cycle begins when we are being lured by an outside temptation and there is an inside lust attracted to that temptation. When we put that together with isolation and the provision to commit the sin, we are in for a raging battle. As the spiritual battle begins, the evil one will seek to make the most of any opportunity. So then, we have an outside allurement and an inside desire with the enemy at work to encourage the great lie: "It's worth it." Little do we realize just how critical this moment is, and who and what is far more valuable and at our disposal—Jesus Christ. (James 1:14a; Ephesians 4:27; 1 Peter 5:8)

2. Feeble struggle: Perhaps we realize that following our desires would be sin. If so, and we are true believers, there is likely a meager attempt to resist or distance ourselves from the opportunity. But if desires and thoughts are not fully dealt with God's way, or sufficient action isn't taken, the temptation remains persistent and grows even stronger. We may even have a thought about how we might escape the temptation, but it is not taken seriously.

3. Rationalization or Rationale: Our flesh is more than eager to offer up rationalizations in the form of excuses or lies in an effort to minimize the seriousness of the sin, justify our giving in or validating the sinful choice. Perhaps the rationale and habit have long since been established. Rationalization gives us a false comfort and a measure of blindness about sin.

Below is only a sample list of rationalizations which are heard in counseling (or used personally!). Do you recognize your rationalizations? Can you add your own?

- I am not hurting anyone else.
- It's not that big of a deal; God understands
- This sin is better than . . .
- I will give it up next time; this will be the last time.
- This is an exception because of exceptional circumstances.
- I want and deserve some comfort, peace and/or pleasure.
- I have no other choice.
- It is a need or only right that . . .
- I have already failed in my mind or heart, so . . .

Now if you are saying, "I don't know what you're talking about," well, you are reading the wrong book! But if you are a believer, and are willing to think about these rationalizations honestly, you will probably agree that in choosing to sin you have taken part in similar excuses fueled by the temporary, personal worship of something other than God. (Luke 16:15)

4. Unholy surrender or feelings of hopelessness: Feelings or thoughts of "I must have that . . ." "I need . . ." "I have to . . ." or "I just can't win" begin to set in. Thoughts about yourself and what you feel reign supreme while God, the deceitfulness of sin and the surpassing value and satisfaction of Christ are overlooked or disregarded. When this happens, we are one small step away from acting against what is holy and right and may even contemplate presuming upon God's grace and forgiveness. We think, *"Aghh! This never-ending struggle!" or "Aghh! This need!" "Surely God will understand and forgive me. He's done it many times before."*(Hebrews 3:13)

5. Sin is carried,out, accompanied by real guilt: This thinking, coupled with the lust in our heart, gives birth to sin in the heart, and then it follows that sin is accomplished (James 1:15). We choose to go ahead and give in to our sin. Whatever it is—overeating, looking at something we shouldn't, spending money foolishly, or something else—we act on the promise and hope of the comfort, satisfaction, validation, or pleasure it will deliver. There is a prevailing shortsightedness that reaches only to what we might momentarily gain. (James 1:15; Jeremiah 51:5)

6. Momentary guilty pleasure or relief: There is usually an immediate, momentary payoff; that passing pleasure of sin; that brief gratification or relief. What was so attractive is so good for a moment, but it is soon accompanied by shame from our guilt, a certain kind of death (leanness of soul) and growing destruction.

7. Sorrow and shame: The consequence of guilt happens immediately when we sin, so very soon we start feeling shame and disgust. *"I can't believe I did that again!"* The pleasure is over, and we are left dealing with the sorrow and effects of sin. Sin is far reaching, even if you don't think so. Again, the evil one will make as much use of our guilt as possible. (Psalm 32:3-4; Revelation 12:10)

8. Confession to God delayed: We think or say to ourselves, "I can't go to God. Not right now. I have sinned against Him, and this is the umpteenth time I've done it!" You decide to wait this one out a little while. You feel so awful that you believe you can't face God. In this state you may slide down the slippery slope of self-pity or depression and on to other means of dealing with your guilt. (1 John 2:28)

9. A type of confession: Time passes, and when you think you have punished yourself enough, or you have experienced even greater pain from the consequences of your sin, you are ready to try talking to God and a type of confession is made. You begin to try and embrace once again Christ's work on the Cross for you. At this point, a measure of hopelessness may linger or you may just plod along with a new resolve, as you try to give it all to God and ask Him to take it all away. You may try to pump yourself up for change, promising better choices in the future. But you can't do it on your own; you are no match for your flesh. (Psalm 51)

10. Christ is not put on and provisions for the flesh are not eliminated: At this point, we are not really dealing with desires and thoughts God's way, nor are we taking drastic measures to avoid temptation, lust and sin. Even more importantly, we are not really treasuring and pursuing who and what is missing from our Christian walk. (Romans 13:14)

11. No outside help is sought: We choose to keep it private. We determine that this must continue to be our own private struggle and we are going to work on it alone. This way, hopefully, no one else will have to know. Everyone else seems to have it all together (though they don't) and we are too embarrassed to admit our struggle. You'll handle it. You haven't been able to do that for years, but you believe you have to try once again. (Galatians 6:1; Proverbs 18:1).

12. Time passes—the perfect set up remains in place: Time goes by and soon it all begins again, because there is still no real change in our focus, our situation or our actions. The lust cycle continues until we are ready to do whatever is necessary to change. Change begins when we learn to value and delight in Christ supremely, and to appropriate the faith and resources God has given us. (1 Corinthians 6:12)

Even though you may know this cycle very well, the hope God hold's out to you is that He and His truth *can* help you break and replace that cycle (2 Peter 1:3-4, Psalm 119:45). And the amazing thing is, that because of God's grace and mercy, even all your past failures can be useful—useful in your growth, to God's people and useful even for God's glory—as long as you repent and begin to *vivify* or quicken and strengthen in your walk today what has been missing all along. (Romans 8:28-29)

> *... knowing this, that our old self was*
> *crucified with him, in order that our body*
> *of sin might be done away with, so that we*
> *should no longer be slaves to sin ...*
> **Romans 6:6 (NASB)**

Chapter 2

Something Is Missing

*For if we have become united with Him in
the likeness of His death, certainly we shall
also be in the likeness of His resurrection . . .
that we should no longer be slaves to sin . . .
Therefore do not let sin reign in your mortal
body so that you should obey its lusts . . .
for sin shall not be master over you,
for you are not under law, but under grace.*
Romans 6:5-14 (NASB)

Our son is an excellent car mechanic. Often he has to trouble-shoot for answers when a car is brought into the shop, looking beyond the obvious damage or malfunction to determine the root cause of the problem. Sometimes, all the work and repair in the world will amount to little without the realization that something crucial is missing: the oil! The creator of the engine designed it to require oil to keep it running smoothly.

Whether you find yourself repeating over and over one of the "respectable sins," or you seem caught in an endless cycle of a particularly grievous sin, not dealing with it God's way has damaging effects on your Christian life. You must determine the root cause of your problem, and just like running a car without the oil, you must ask yourself not what is happening, but what is missing. It is crucial to know what God has to say about the role of the Gospel in your fight against sin. Learning these truths can make all the difference in really laying hold of the resources God has for you, for His glory.

Conquering sin habits means doing them mortal harm in an all out battle, in the strength of Christ! A sort of lost but good word is "mortify."[1] The word mortify is not common in our language these days, but it was used in the King James Version of the Bible. One definition of mortify in the Merriam Webster Collegiate Dictionary is "to destroy the strength, vitality, and functioning of," in this case, a particular sin.[2] It is based on the biblical Greek word, *thanatŏō*, which basically means *to "put to death" or kill* (Romans 8:13).[3]

An old puritan pastor, John Owen, is a friend to your struggle. His books on this subject made a great impact in his day. He very carefully laid out God's principles for killing a sin habit. Though the language of his writings is a bit strange for us today, in them you will find a very important word for us. John Owen never taught mortifying sin (putting it off) without teaching on what he called "vivification," (putting something on) which for our topic, involves a putting on of the truest and most altering replacements for our sin. Though this booklet is about finally putting to death your sin habit, the first thing you need to know is that you can't just kill or even control sin.

---

[1]   The Biblical teaching of "Mortifying sin in your life" was made popular back in the Puritan era by John Owen. Owen was probably the most prolific writer on the subject of mortifying sin. Volume Six, *Sin and Temptation*, in his multi-volume series, *The Works of John Owen*, is a biblical theology of sin and its effects in our life. John Owen, *Sin and Temptation*, Minneapolis, MN: Bethany House Publishers, 1996.

[2]   Miriam Webster Collegiate Dictionary, 10th addition. Miriam Webster Incorporation, Springfield Mass, 1993, ed in chief: Fredrick C. Mish

[3]   Cleon L.Rogers Jr. and Cleon L.Rogers III. *The New Linguistic and Exegetical Key to the Greek New Testament.* Grand Rapids: Zondervan Publishing House. 1998, 330.

This is often the greater focus of 12 step programs and other counseling help.

The fact is, you cannot kill sin without a full replacement of it with something else; with the *right* things. The most fundamental thing to activate at the right time, in the right way is *faith*. So in a sense, as strange as it may sound to you, the title of this book could be "Mortify Sin; Vivify Your Faith in Christ."

Vivify means to endue with life, or to quicken. It is about bringing to life or making something more effective or perhaps effective in a new way. But let me be clear, it is not just about doing something, it is about being something or personally embracing something from the inside out—for the glory it brings to God and the eternal kind of life it brings to us.

Just as the mechanic must infuse oil into the engine of the car for true restoration and usefulness, we must really lay hold of what is missing. With this book, we want to help you vivify in your life that which will allow you, in light of Christ and the Gospel, to mortify the sin that entangles or gets the best of you. If daily vivification doesn't happen in the Christian life, the end is always fleshly (selfish, worldly) living. Everything that you need to vivify is very connected to your faith in Christ. In light of this truth, every Christian needs to vivify "killer-faith" to subdue and overcome the destructive lust cycle in their lives. We will see how we do this in the next chapter.

I have been crucified with Christ.
It is no longer I who live, but Christ who
lives in me. And the life I now live in the
flesh I live by faith in the Son of God,
who loved me and gave himself for me.
Galatians 2:20

If there is one darling sin that you would
spare, Christ and your soul will never agree.
There can be no peace between you and Christ
while there is peace between you and sin.
Charles Spurgeon

Chapter 3

Context Is Everything!

Perhaps you know someone who loves to garden. For me it is my mother. Sometimes she gets up at the crack of dawn to weed and cultivate her flower beds before the heat of the day. She would tell you that without the proper amount of water, nutrients and sun, her labors would be futile. In the same way, moving forward to lay hold of freedom in Christ without the most basic and life-changing environment is like trying to grow plants in crusty, nutrient-stripped ground.

The context for our understanding, and our efforts concerning the killing of a particular sin pattern, must be cultivating Gospel-faith in Jesus Christ. His sacrifice, your salvation, who you are in Him and where you are ultimately headed are the most crucial realities in which to immerse yourself. Because of the Gospel, the killing of the sin that seems to master you is both essential and possible! You are not the exception. It is both possible and imperative for you to have victory because of the Gospel of Jesus!

No Longer Slaves of Sin

If we are commanded to mortify and be free from the mastery of sin, would God not give us the means to do so? He tells us that as believers, we are no longer under the power of sin as we once were.

For the law of the Spirit of life has
set you free in Christ Jesus
from the law of sin and death.
Romans 8:2

This fact is true because as believers Christ is in us and we are in Him (1 John 5:20; John 14:20; Romans 6:4-7, 14). We have the power to overcome sin His way, because we have His power in us at our disposal (Romans 8:9-11, Philippians 2:13). Though we may choose to walk in the flesh and thereby voluntarily place ourselves back under its control, we do not have to do so. If we belong to Christ and call on the power of the Holy Spirit in faith, His strength is sufficient. And, we will learn later just what it means to walk by the Spirit rather than the flesh and the difference it can make in our lives.

Our Debt of Love and Obedience

It is in understanding the cost of our undeserved rescue from hell, sin and self that we grasp the magnitude of our debt of love and obedience (1 Corinthians 6:19-20; Luke 7:41-47). We have been reconciled forever with the God of faithfulness! We are taught in Romans how unthinkable it is to let sin reign in us in light of the Gospel—in light of the fact that we have been forgiven and are in union with Christ. Romans 6:15 says, **"So what then? Are we to sin because we are not under law but under grace? By no means!"** Instead, the love of Christ and the Gospel gives us the right motivation for victory over our sin habits. As we remember that we were sought by God, then forgiven and reconciled through a suffering Savior, the glad obligation and compulsion to please Him rises up within us. We are raised to a new identity and newness of life with Him and are headed to eternity with the Lord of all creation! Christ's person, mercy and love deserve a genuine change in our direction, and if we really see what He has done for us, it will be a change we desire to make (Romans 6:1-11; John 6:37-40).

> *So then, brothers, we are debtors, not to the*
> *flesh, to live according to the flesh.*
> *For if you [keep on] live[ing] according to*
> *the flesh you will die, but if by the Spirit you*
> *[keep on]put[ting] to death the*
> *deeds of the body, you will live.*
> *Romans 8:12-13*
> *[Greek verb tense]*

> *For the love of Christ controls us, because*
> *we have concluded this: that one has died for*
> *all, therefore all have died; and he died for*
> *all, that those who live might no longer live*
> *for themselves but for him who for their sake*
> *died and was raised.*
> *2 Corinthians 5:14-15*

So, the only hope for change from the inside out is to first be changed by the grace of God—to be a person who is reconciled with God; one who is in union with God through faith in Jesus Christ. Are you sure that you have a reconciled relationship with the one true triune God through His Son Jesus Christ? If so, then you understand why you were saved *from* your sin (not saved to continue *in* your sin); to know Him, to treasure Him supremely and to honor Him as His own child and possession forever—all for His glory and your great good.

For the grace of God has appeared,
bringing salvation for all people,
training us to renounce ungodliness
and worldly passions,
and to live self-controlled, upright,
and godly lives in the present age,
waiting for our blessed hope,
the appearing of the glory of our
great God and Savior Jesus Christ,
who gave himself for us to redeem us
from all lawlessness and to
purify for himself a people for his own
possession who are zealous for good works.
Titus 2:11-14

The Hope that Purifies

But we were not saved to know Him, be satisfied in Him and glorify Him here in this life only. The ultimate goal of our salvation is Heaven—where all battle with sin will be finished! Every day, and at the time of every temptation, we should remember that *this* may be the day we see Him face to face. either by his return or by our death,

Beloved we are God's children now
and what we will be has not yet
appeared. We know that when he
appears we shall be like him,
because we shall see him just as he is,
and everyone who has this
hope fixed on him purifies himself,
just as he is pure.
1 John 3: 2-3 (NASB)

Having an eternal perspective is both necessary and purifying. This aspect of the Gospel (our salvation) is crucial for you daily. Remembering that at any moment Christ may return, and hoping in the rest and joy of Christ and heaven, can affect your choices and make a great difference in mortifying your sin.

The verses above are not saying that we will not sin or that we have no sin. Instead, they show that believers must be willing (with their focus on Christ and His strength) to do what He says to do about their sin. In gratitude and expectation, Christians are zealous to live out the life for which He saved them. They understand that they are called to a grace-filled life, basking in His forgiveness, adoption and power, and the hope of Heaven. But they are also called to a surrendered life, in which they seek to honor Jesus Christ.

> The difference between an unconverted and
> a converted man, is not that one has sins and
> the other has none. But the one takes part with
> his cherished sins against a dreaded God and
> the other takes part with his reconciled God
> against his hated sins.
> William Arnot[4]

Moving Forward

"But how," you say, "does this perspective and desire actually work itself out in my life, when a pattern of sin has been established? How can I win over habitual sin for Christ's sake? Why don't I seem to be able to have victory?" Well, there may be several reasons. But first of all, you must ask yourself, do you really, whole heartedly, want to put off sin, because of all

---

[4] William Arnot. *Laws from Heaven for Life on Earth*, 311.

He has done for you and because you grasp the ultimate goal of your salvation (eternity with Him)? (Psalm 66:18)

If you have answered 'yes' to these questions, then you are ready to take this to God and learn how to appropriate His truth and walk in liberty with Him. Generally speaking, this brings us back to what John Owen has taught us: Victory for Christ will be realized only by vivifying (bringing to life) that which is missing in our relationship and walking with Him. Our sin is largely a result of what is *not* true in our lives. Your faith will not be spirit-enabled *killer faith* without the vivification of the Gospel in your daily life (Colossians 3:1-10).

First and foremost you must bring to life more of a Gospel perspective each day; remembering what Christ has done for you, the power that is within you and where you are headed. The more you treasure the Gospel and all that it really means, the more it will affect your desires and your actions. The more you trust and treasure your *union* with Christ, the more it will affect your *communion* (or practical walk) with Him. Now let's explore what else you need to vivify!

Chapter 4

Exercise (Vivify) Daily Christian Faith

I'd like to tell you about a man we will call Joe. Joe is a professing believer and a member of a church-sponsored support group. He has struggled with his "sex addiction" for over 12 years. He attends his group meeting every week, along with several others who have similar problems. They talk about their struggles with sin, confess to each other and count the days since they last gave in to their particular sin. They also have a plan for how to hold each other accountable, so that they might not yield to sin. This would seem to cover everything they should do, but you see, that is all they do. As well-meaning as Joe and the other members of his 12 step group are, they are not engaged in biblical sanctification. It is great if they do not succumb to the sin they are trying to overcome, but if Joe is not seeing the importance of exercising practical faith in his fight, then he is involved in a losing battle.

It takes faith in Christ to be reconciled to a right relationship with God. It also takes exercising our faith to live the Christian life in light of the challenges and temptations of each day. All the promises and realities in God and the Gospel should have an impact on what we are doing and what we are thinking (2 Peter 1:3-4). We need to make active our faith at crucial times of trial, temptation and sin. Choosing to be a person of faith at times of temptation will grow your faith and make a fundamental difference in your ability to resist temptation and mortify your sin. You must recognize the times when you are not exercising faith. Even though our faith was made alive at salvation, we may not be exercising it when we should be (1 Timothy 4:7-10). All that is true about our God, and made true for us through the Gospel of Christ needs to come to life when we are troubled, tempted, or we sin. Amazingly, this kind of childlike faith works to help subdue sinful deeds in our lives and enable us to have victory through the power of the Holy Spirit.

> *. . . let us draw near with a true heart in full assurance of faith, with our hearts sprinkled clean from an evil conscience and our bodies washed with pure water. Let us hold fast the confession of our hope without wavering, for he who promised is faithful.*
> *Hebrews 10:22-23*

Realities to Exercising Faith

We are sinning when we do not choose to exercise our faith in times of temptation, and that is the beginning and the furtherance of our downfall. Ask God to help you to grow in your faith. Ask Him to make you aware of times when you need to turn to Him in faith. Ask Him to strengthen your faith, as you seek to exercise it. Have faith to believe He will because he has declared Himself to be the rewarder of those who truly seek Him and His way (Hebrews 11:6). Exercising your faith means that belief, thankfulness, dependence, and/or confidence concerning the realities of Christ and the Gospel are present. The simple prayer that begins, "Lord I thank you that . . ." can refocus us with faith and make a huge difference at critical times. Here is a list of realities that we must turn to and exercise our faith in daily:

- Christ is the maker and Lord of all creation, yet He was willing to suffer such condescension, humiliation, divine and human rejection and torture for my rescue and reconciliation—all demonstrating that *He* is the only Savior, the Good Shepherd, the Bread of Life, the True Vine, the Fountain of Living Water, and the True Refuge I need. (Philippians 2:9-11; Colossians 1:13-22; John 10:11; John 6:35; John 15:1; Jeremiah 2:13; John 4:13-14; Psalm 46:1)

- I am forgiven and have an advocate (the Savior) who pleads my case on the basis of His sinless life, the rejection and wrath of God poured out on Him, and His death on the cross for my sin. (Colossians 1:14; Romans 5:6-10; 1 John 2:1-2)

- I am eternally justified and adopted through Christ's substitutionary death. (Romans 5:9-10; Ephesians 1:5-8)

- I am indwelt with all the power of the Holy Spirit in Christ, because of the Cross! I can call on God's powerful assistance through Christ. (Romans 8: 9-11; Philippians 2:13)

- By faith in Christ's work on the cross, I died with Christ and died to the power (slavery) of sin. Because of that I can choose to be dead to my love of and service to sin and alive to God—a slave of righteousness. (Romans 6)

- I am set by God on a sure path of being conformed into the image of Christ. This *will* continue and be perfected (end at glorification), by God's will and purpose—no matter how bad it looks now (Romans 8:28; Philippians 1:6; Jude 1:24). Though I stumble, I will not utterly fall, "because the Lord is the one who holds [my] hand." (Psalm 37:24)

- My old life, and who I was (as a whole), has passed away and a new person has come through Christ. Positionally (in my standing with God) this is already a reality. And, it is also true in that I am fundamentally given a new identity, a new kind of heart that desires to and can please Him, a new future and even a new past (forgiven, understandable, useful). These things are true, even though I still have the flesh to contend with, and *do* need more practical heart and life change. I am still becoming all that I am and will be in Christ when I reach Heaven. (2 Corinthians 5:17-18, Ephesians 2:1-10; Romans 8:28-39)

- I am united with Christ—He in me and I in Him—and nothing can separate me from the love of Christ. (1 John 5:20; John 14:20; Romans 8:38-39)

- I am bought /purchased with a great price! Because of that I am gladly not my own. I am privileged to embrace the debt of love and obedience I owe to the one who gave *all* for me and to the one who demonstrated the depth of love He has for me. (1 Corinthians 6:19-20; Hebrews 12:28)

- God is great enough and faithful enough to work all things together for my good and my growth into His likeness. He has promised this to me until I reach Heaven. He has predestined and declared my good and my growth. God is always *for* me because of the cross, no matter what life's circumstances look like. He is always making useful every trial (even Satan's schemes and my failures). He is using them to conform me into His image, draw me to Himself, be God to me and truly bless me. (Romans 8:28-39; Philippians 1:6; Psalm 73:23; 1 Thessalonians 5:23-24)

- Jesus Christ is coming back. I will see Him face to face; review my life, but also rest in His love and grace. I will finally be without sin, wholly loving Him and being loved by Him forever. (2 Corinthians 5:9-10; 2 John 1:8; Romans 8:18-23; 1 Corinthians 13:12; Revelation 21:3-5)

In order to exercise faith in these truths when we need them, they must be on our minds and in our hearts—or at least readily available! These are the realities that every believer should regularly be walking in and rehearsing. You would do well to review the verses found in this list and meditate on them daily. Write down those you seem to forget, along with Scripture on an index card and use them when you are lacking in your faith. Just as daily physical exercise builds strong muscles, rehearsing these Gospel realities will strengthen your faith, and it will make a difference in your efforts to put to death sin in your life.

Faith and Repentance

Genuine repentance *with faith* is crucial in the mortification of your sin. Sincere confession and making an authentic turn back to Christ in faith should actually be a regular occurrence for the believer, because we sin often. Our fall into that same old sin usually comes well after failing to recognize other, earlier times when we were not having faith or we did not repent with faith. True repentance means a full turn from our sin, through faith, *to something*—Christ and His way. The fact that we keep repeating the same sin is a sign that our "repentance" was only worldly sorrow that stops short of a real turning, or that it was lacking a robust remembrance and revived focus on the realities of Christ and the Gospel.

Confession is the beginning of repentance. A true confession must involve seeing sin as an offense against a holy God and a grief to the Savior. It must also involve a desire and intent to change. Then, if confession is accompanied by faith, it is not a negative thing, but a glorious, much needed thing. Confession should not be distained, avoided or lead to discouragement with the thought, "But here I am again!" While it is definitely not good that you are where you are when confession is needed, the faith involved in a Christ focused confession is both honoring to God and restoring and life-changing for you.

In his book, *How People Change,* Jay Adams discusses the conviction of sin by the Holy Spirit. In a lengthy discussion he explains how confession is in essence the gate that leads to true repentance.[5] And that is true, so long as it is accompanied by faith that is true. When we confess having faith in God's promises it turns us back to the person of Christ and allows us to carry out full repentance. One most important promise is that we have an advocate with the Father (Christ) pleading our case on the basis of His death, so we can be forgiven (1 John 1:9)

> *. . . let the wicked forsake his way,*
> *and the unrighteous man his thoughts;*
> *let him return to the Lord, that he may have*
> *compassion on him, and to our God,*
> *for he will abundantly pardon.*
> *Isaiah 55:7*

True confession (and repentance) means that we recognize our decision to sin is a move *away* from our Savior; our Lord; the only true hope. So, a faith-filled confession of

---

5   Jay Adams, *How People Change*, (Grand Rapids, MI: Zondervan, 1986), 107-132.

sin is one that once again sees Christ for who He is, trusts the truths of the Gospel and values both more than sin. This recognition is the first thing we need in order to move out of a fleshly state. It is important to deal with all past sin God's way and clear our conscience, or this kind of return is not possible. You may need help from a godly person to work through your past biblically. Just remember that there is nothing God's grace can't cover and there is nothing He and His truth cannot help you work through and move beyond. Sometimes we turn to certain sins as a refuge because we are running from our past.[6]

It is crucial to remember that after you've sinned you can still glorify God. A faith-filled confession and turn away from sin gives great glory to God. Acknowledging that our heart has turned from Him to worthless, broken cisterns (leaky ancient water pots or futile things we set our focus, desires and hopes on), brings God glory. Confession of our sinful act for what it is glorifies Him. Acknowledging and embracing Him once again in faith brings Him the glory He deserves. And, doing everything to go fully in the direction of what is right and good instead brings glory to God too (illustrated in Joshua 7:19-20).

> ***Then Joshua said to Achan, "My son, give glory to the Lord God of Israel and give praise to him. And tell me now what you have done; do not hide it from me." And Achan answered Joshua, "Truly I have sinned against the Lord God of Israel, and this is what I did . . . .***

---

[6] Steve Viars' book, *Putting Your Past in its Place,* can be very helpful in sorting through one's past and moving beyond it to the newness of life with Christ available in him. (Eugene: OR, Harvest House *Publisher, 2011).*

Full repentance is a grace of God for which we should pray (2 Timothy 2:25). It is a work of God's Spirit, influencing a personal choice whereby we are inwardly humbled and visibly reformed. It is made up of five spiritual ingredients (adapted from a list in *The Doctrine of Repentance* by Thomas Watson):

1. Sight of sin (against the perfections of Christ)

2. Sorrow and shame for sin (in light of Christ and the Gospel)

3. Confession of sin (turning back to Christ and the cross)

4. Hatred for sin (as Christ does)

5. Turning from sin to a beautiful pursuit (Christ and His way)[7]

Genuine and complete repentance will *always* involve exercising faith. The two must never be separated. In faith, we choose to trust God's view of sin and what is right, not our own interpretation. In faith, we must wholly trust His amazing grace, forgiveness and love, all because of the cross. And in faith we set our hopes and desires fully back on Christ and Heaven (1 Peter 1:13; Psalm 73:25-28). Will you choose to confess unbelief or a lack of trust and pursue being a person of faith?

---

[7] Thomas Watson, *The Doctrine of Repentance*. (Carlisle, PA: The Banner of Truth Trust. 1668 (1994), 18-58. This list has been adapted to our topic and reduced from six to five points; sorrow and shame having been combined.

Chapter 5

Vivify a Right Priority!

It is no secret that we are all prone to reverse the priority of very important things in our lives! In the Scriptures, God cautions us to keep the first things first because it is always crucial to our good and His glory. This truth leads us to the second thing that must be vivified in our endeavor to mortify sin. A proper emphasis is needed between what we are pursuing and what we are trying to stop, but we must also determine a proper priority among all the right pursuits. If not, we will end up doing things in our own strength, and become legalistic and give up.

Perhaps some examples would be helpful here. I am to love my wife Zondra "as Christ loved the Church" (Ephesians 5:25). Wow! That is an immense task! Even so, Jesus said that my love for Him must be so great that it looks like I "hate" Zondra in comparison (Luke 14:26). When I don't maintain this priority, my Christian walk does not go well! Another example is found in Luke 10:38-42 where Martha misplaced her strong concern for hospitality, causing her to put off the most important priority of sitting and listening to Jesus' words.

Let's look at three specific priorities you must pursue with all you've got, but don't lose sight of the fact that your most important priority must be Christ Himself. We will examine each of these in their proper order.

1. The Priority of the Surpassing Value of Christ: First and foremost, there must be a focus, a pursuit, a valuing of the person of Christ. The only thing more worthy, more valuable and more satisfying than your sin is Him! In fact, I can say with confidence that you are in this battle against sin because you were not focused on Christ for all that He is, nor are you worshiping and enjoying Him for it. Unless we see the surpassing value of Christ, and therefore see all else as rubbish or broken cisterns, we will worship something else (Philippians 3:8). We are created worshipers and are always worshiping something. So, most of all, we must seek to know, treasure, depend on, and enjoy Christ more (Psalm 73: 25-28; Colossians 1:16-18). This is fundamentally what is missing or at least far too minimal in our lives. It is, of course, inherently tied to the faith we discussed in chapters 3 and 4 and should involve the Triune God as a whole: Father, Son and Holy Spirit.

The first thing we must do to worship Christ more is to recognize and confess what we have been treasuring and worshiping instead. Seeing your misplaced worship and trust as spiritual adultery and idol worship is key. About Israel, who worshipped and trusted in other things, God said:

> *Son of man, these men have set up their idols*
> *in their hearts and have put right before their*
> *faces the stumbling block of their iniquity...*
> *I the LORD will be brought to give him an*
> *answer in the matter in view of the multitude*
> *of his idols, in order to lay hold of the hearts*
> *of the house of Israel who are estranged*
> *from Me through all their idols."'*
> *Ezekiel 14: 3-5 (NASB)*

What are the things that you tend to take refuge in or worship as an idol? They are the things you sin to get, sin if you don't get and/or turn to when troubled. As you repent and commit to forsake those things for Christ, you must begin to put your focus and hope solely back on who Christ really is. Here are some ways you can do that:

- Read and meditate on the four Gospels and the book of Psalms in the Bible. This will help you cultivate a greater love for Christ.
- Contemplate on Christ's life, His sacrifice and His present activities for you. This will surely lead you to worship.
- Study and review the names and attributes of Christ or the Triune God as a whole. This will also help increase your devotion.
- Begin spending time in personal worship through prayer and song. You will be more likely to value Christ as you should.

2. The Priority of Walking by the Spirit: Another related driving purpose that must be present is that of *walking by or in the Spirit*. As a Christian you should be a person who is in the habit of walking in the Spirit, though you will not do it perfectly in this life. Clearly, the greatest aspect of walking by the Spirit is what has just been discussed, but there is more. This walking by the Spirit is put another way in Ephesians 5: 18 when we are told to "be filled with the Spirit." It can be further explained by Colossians 3:1-4 and 6-17, and Ephesians 3:16 with Isaiah 40:31 as: (1) letting the word of Christ dwell richly within us, (2) pursuing Scripture-filled relationships with other Christians, (3) seeking to serve an ever-present Christ and His interests with thankfulness and (4) desperately depending on His power, rather than on our own strength. Here's what God has to say about the importance of walking by the Spirit, where your sinful desires and passions are concerned:

> **But I say, walk by the Spirit, and you**
> **will not gratify the desires of the flesh.**
> **Galatians 5:16**

You see, the next verse tells us, ". . . for the flesh sets its desire against the Spirit, and Spirit against the flesh; for these are in opposition to one another, so that you may not do the things that you please" (Galatians 5:17, NASB). But the good news in verse eighteen is that because the power of sin over you has been broken, if you are "being led by" (following after) the things of the Spirit, you will not foolishly place yourself again under the sway of the "law" of the flesh (Galatians 5:18; Romans 7:23).

Practically speaking, to the degree that you are pursuing the things of the Spirit, this is the degree to which your flesh is weakened. In fact, it is virtually impossible to serve the flesh at the same time that you are, in dependence, having a God and others focus, or while letting the Word of God "dwell richly within you" with thankfulness. Don't miss this: when you are walking by the Spirit, you won't gratify the desires of the flesh! So in addition to your pursuit of Christ and all that is in Him, here is how you can proactively be walking by the Spirit:

- *Letting the Word of God dwell richly within you.* The Spirit uses the Word of God to work in our hearts and lives in whatever ways are needed (John 17:17). Because this is true, it is imperative that you put yourself in its path in every way possible and meditate on how it relates to you. Read Psalm 19:7-11 and Psalm 119 to see what the Word of God can accomplish in conjunction with the Spirit. Consider the following:

For the word of God is living and active,
sharper than any two-edged sword,
piercing to the division of soul and of spirit,
of joints and of marrow, and discerning
the thoughts and intentions of the heart.
Hebrews 4:12

- *Having open and refining relationships.* It is interesting that in both Colossians 3 and Ephesians 5, where being filled with the Spirit and being filled with the Word are discussed, we have the exhortation to keep on encouraging and keep on admonishing (in love) one another with the Word. This is not possible if we are not being open with one another about our discouragements and sin struggles. Hopefully you are in a church environment where this is encouraged and practiced. If not, it may be time for a change. Begin seeking out friends and mentors who will join you in your pursuit of Christ, encourage you in your battle against sin and pray for you. While it is neither wise nor needed to tell all to everyone, Proverbs 18:1 gives you a critical warning concerning your freedom from sin:

Whoever isolates himself seeks his own
desire; he breaks out against
all sound judgment.
Proverbs 18:1

- *Serving God and others, with thankfulness.* Again, in the Colossians and Ephesians passages, serving God (and therefore others) and thankfulness are both highlighted (Colossians 3:1-17; Ephesians 5:18-21). The two go hand in hand. It is impossible to sin against Christ while you are being thankful for who He is and what He has done for you. You will be grateful for His perpetual love and grace and the new identity He has given you. Keep a thankful list with you and add to it daily. This kind of thankfulness should drive a crucial new aim—that of serving God and others wherever you are. Setting your mind on serving God and others is another key element of walking in the Spirit rather than the flesh. This is true because you will not be focused on yourself! But most importantly, having a God and others focus glorifies God because it is being like Christ (John 4:34; Philippians 2: 1-8).

. . . whatever you do, in word or deed, do everything in the name of the Lord Jesus, giving thanks to God the Father . . .
Colossians 3:17

• *Depending on the Spirit.* To walk in the Spirit also means to depend on the Spirit's help for everything. In faith, you must believe that His help and grace are more than sufficient (Hebrews 4:16; 2 Corinthians 9:8; 2 Corinthians 12: 9). Christ says, "…apart from me you can do nothing [that glorifies God and lasts]" but also, "[you] can do all things through Him who strengthens [you]" (John 15:5, Philippians 4:13). In Romans 6 Paul talks about our "position in Christ." In Romans 7 (also Galatians 5:17), he writes about the ongoing conflict and struggle Christians face in their battle against the flesh. The solution is found in Romans 8 where Paul tells us how we are to walk this Christian life. Throughout these passages, Paul refers to the Holy Spirit twenty times. Putting sin to death cannot be done in your own strength, but by that of the Holy Spirit of God. God, through the pen of Paul, is trying to make the point that you can't live the Christian life, from the inside out, without the Spirit of God empowering you. Admitting your need and asking for God's strength takes humility, but it also empowers you and honors God. If you truly get this aspect of walking by the Spirit, there will be a lot of prayer going on! Ask God to help you to become a more praying, dependent child of His—to "pray without ceasing" (1 Thessalonians 5:17). If you are being thankful, are practicing His presence and acknowledging your need, you will be!

> *Devote yourselves to prayer, keeping alert in*
> *it with an attitude of thanksgiving.*
> *Colossians 4:2 (NASB)*

As you begin your day, pray and determine to walk in the Spirit by putting yourself in the path of his Word (hear, read, meditate on it), being involved with other strong believers, setting out to serve God and others, and asking for the Spirit's help.

3. The Priority of the Righteous Alternative: In addition to centralizing *the surpassing value of Christ* and purposing to *walk in the Spirit,* you must also begin to think more about the *righteous alternative(s)* to your sin than on the sin you wish to avoid. In fact, circling around the sin and the dreaded pit of failure will create more temptation and lead to falling in! Remember, the object is to move as far away from that pit as possible by putting on the character of what is right. So whatever the sin is, search the Scriptures to determine what the opposite, Christ-like attitude or behavior is and begin praying about it and pursuing it aggressively. For example, Ephesians 4:22-32 teaches us that the righteous alternative to deceit is pursuing truth and openness, the righteous alternative to stealing is to work and be a giver, the righteous alternative to destructive speech is seeking to be a person who builds others up and speaks with grace, and the righteous alternative to anger and bitterness is kindness, tenderheartedness and forgiveness. Valuing and aggressively pursuing the Christlike, corresponding characteristic to whatever you are dealing with will make an effective difference in mortifying your sin. Enlist help here if you are not sure what the alternative would be.

If you think about it, just working to stop or put off your sin has not been enough for lasting change. Certainly, there are some specific things to stop and implement where your temptations and sins are concerned. But without these more important priorities (especially *the* priority of Christ Himself), your own efforts will not take you far in your battle against sin. Nor will you be glorifying God and walking with Him as He intended. So, which of these very important priorities do you need to ask God to help you vivify and develop most? Begin today to purposefully move in that direction!

Chapter 6

Vivify Spiritual Exercise!

I like to run, well . . . I actually jog. In the world of running there is a difference between the two. I have been jogging cross country since high school. I learned early in this endeavor to believe the axiom that *the more you are faithful and consistent, the better you will be.* Even now, when I am sick or have to travel and can't exercise I can see how quickly I regress. Ask anyone who has ever exercised in any manner and they will tell you it is hard to get into shape, easy to get out of it and so it is best to maintain and stay in it.

Whether you physically exercise your heart and body or not, you are probably at least aware that you should—now—and that you should *keep doing it* for best results. There is also another kind of heart exercise we need to consider and maintain. That is the all-important spiritual kind.

Now that we have discussed important personal priorities and we have seen the need to respond to the Gospel with action, it is important for us to know clearly what our role and God's role are in the growth process. A proper theology of sanctification (growth and change) as it relates to our own effort will facilitate our freedom for God's glory. To reiterate an important point, we begin this topic with the reminder that any effort we put into our Christian walk must be done because we *already have* Christ, His love and forgiveness and not in order to attain them.

> *. . . yet we know that a person*
> *is not justified by works of the law but*
> *through faith in Jesus Christ, so we also*
> *have believed in Christ Jesus, in order*
> *to be justified by faith in Christ and not*
> *by works of the law, because by works of the*
> *law no one will be justified.*
> **Galatians 2:16**

The ultimate motivation for us to vivify spiritual exercise
in our lives is the same as that of *exercising your faith* and
having the right priority—Gratitude!

> *For to this end we toil and strive,*
> *because we have our hope set on the*
> *living God, who is the Savior of all people,*
> *especially of those who believe.*
> **1 Timothy 4:10**

> *Or do you presume on the riches of his*
> *kindness and forbearance and patience,*
> *not knowing that God's kindness is meant*
> *to lead you to repentance?*
> **Romans 2:4**

To be clear, we are not doing our part *for* God's
acceptance, but *because* we have it.

The Participants in Your Change

The key player, and the One who gets all the credit for our growth
and change (sanctification), is of course, God (Philippians
1:6; 1 Thessalonians 5:23-24). The Father is orchestrating all
things for our learning and our good and is blessing us in ways
we tend not to recognize (Romans 8:28-29). The Holy Spirit

convicts and is willing to impart His mighty power to both carry out God's will and endure hardship (Philippians 2:13; Ephesians 3:16). He also prays for us, leads us in what is right, and comforts us (Romans 8:26; John 16:7-14; Acts 9:31). Jesus Christ accomplished our salvation and is standing for us as our advocate when we sin. He is also praying for us, and has led us by example as He Himself is our ultimate goal (Romans 8:34; 1 Peter 2:21; Philippians 3:12-14).

The Scriptures are clear that *we* play a role too. All God asks of us is that we co-operate with Him in what He is seeking to do (mold us after the pattern of Christ) in our lives. God has clearly communicated that there should be intentional effort in both areas of our life—heart and behavior—to become a person more like Christ. He has told *us* to worship Him only and be renewed in the spirit of our minds, while also to add… to [our] faith various godly characteristics, make no provision for the flesh, and pursue the many means of grace He has given (i.e., the Word, prayer, etc.—Luke 4:8; Ephesians 4:23; 2 Peter 1:5-11; Romans 13:14; Romans 8:12-13; 1 Timothy 4:7-10). And let's not forget that He has even commanded us to "put on" the fruit of the Spirit and the new self, and "put to death" the deeds of the flesh by putting off the old self (Colossians 3:12; Ephesians 4:23-24; Colossians 3:5). Though these are in a real sense by–products of God's grace, they are also all areas in which God expects us to make effort. Doing these things from a heart of gratitude unto Christ, and through dependence on His power, is different from attempting to nail fruit on a dead or root–damaged tree apart from God's power.[8] They are different because when they are done from a dependent heart of faith and worship, they flow from His power and *are* worship themselves (Romans 12:1).

---

[8]   Paul D.Tripp. *Instruments in the Redeemer's Hands*, (Phillipsburg, NJ: P&R Publishers, 2002), 63.

We must not expect God to do all the work for us, but take very seriously our dependent and co-operative role. In at least two places in the writings of Paul, we see clear statements concerning God's perspective on our responsibility of effort. Clearly, God will not obey for you. Change is a matter of dependence on His power with your response of effort.

Therefore, my beloved, as you have always obeyed, so now, not only as in my presence but much more in my absence, work out your own salvation with fear and trembling, for it is God who works in you, both to will and to work for his good pleasure.
Philippians 2:12-13

For this I toil, struggling with all his energy that he powerfully works within me.
Colossians 1:29

So we must not only ask, "What am I worshiping and what truth do I need to speak to my heart in faith?" but also, "What Christ-like quality do I need to pursue and what zealous action do I need to take for Christ, with His help?" We should not expect (because God doesn't) that even a right heart will easily or automatically flow into all the right actions, especially where those strong habits exist. When mortifying sin, it is imperative that we employ effort and the practical ways God has given to facilitate change. You must in light of His grace, learn to trust God's power, but also go against feelings and exercise yourself unto godliness with dependent holy sweat!

*Have nothing to do with irreverent silly
myths. Rather train [gymnadzo-exercise]
yourself for godliness; for while bodily
training is of some value, godliness is of
value in every way, as it holds promise for the
present life and also for the life to come.
This saying is trustworthy and
deserving of full acceptance.
1 Timothy 4:7-9*

Specific Exercises

Here are four specific and critical exercises we must employ until, with God's help, they become a part of our daily lives.

1. Renew the mind: A key way to exercise yourself unto godliness and obey the command to "let the word of God dwell in you richly" is by renewing your thoughts with God's truth and doing your part to change wrong thought patterns (Colossians 3:16; Romans 12: 2; Philippians 4:8). We must desire to become a person who has the Word in us that speaks truth to our heart, because it glorifies God and it will help us to be more like Him. So it becomes necessary and crucial that you isolate all you're thinking and beliefs (surrounding your past, circumstances or sin) that need to be renewed and consistently replaced. Repentance will mean preparing new truth-filled thoughts to turn to the next time you are tempted with the old ones (Ephesians 4:22-24). With confession and this active repentance of prayerfully turning to God's truth, you can in time fully replace even very ingrained thought patterns and responses. As you are faithful to turn from the old thoughts and embrace God's truth in the moments that count, the Word of God can begin to "dwell richly within you" where it hasn't been. It is very important to enlist any help needed in mining from the Scriptures all that will help you to renew a particular thought or belief. Keep index cards of your new thoughts and verses with you for quick reference when it is difficult to think rightly. Your pattern of sin must be cut off at the thought level!

> *Do not be conformed to this world,*
> *but be transformed by the renewal of*
> *your mind, that by testing you may discern*
> *what is the will of God, what is good*
> *and acceptable and perfect.*
> *Romans 12:2*

2. Make no provision for the flesh and abstain from fleshly lusts: Concerning sinful habit patterns, the Lord wants us to flee temptation and avoid giving the flesh any opportunity in our particular sin arena. As we strive to become more like Christ, we must be zealous to remove anything that habitually leads us to temptation and also to set up hindrances to sin. As we embrace the sufficiency of God, the goodness of His way, and His plan of molding us, we will want to do away with anything that affects our walk with Him or stands in the way of being like Him.

> *But put on the Lord Jesus Christ and*
> *make no provision for the flesh to*
> *gratify its desires.*
> *Romans 13:14*

> *Beloved, I urge you as sojourners and exiles*
> *to abstain from the passions of the flesh,*
> *which rage war against your soul.*
> *1 Peter 2:11*

If we don't honor these biblical commands, we are not really serious about repentance for Christ; we are already displeasing the Lord and we are setting ourselves up for failure. There may be some things that we must simply abstain from because they quickly turn to serving our lusts. These things might not even be evil in and of themselves. For example, if at this time just seeing the television is a source of temptation towards sexual sin or wasting huge blocks of time, don't have one in the house or put it away! It's not worth it. Or, there may be some things that are fine for others to engage in but not you. It is better to accept this limitation with a thankful heart (in light of all Christ gave up for you) rather than make provision for your flesh. Keep in mind that the provisions you may need to do away with are particular to your own walk and battle with sin and not to be imposed on others. Making no provision and abstaining are two ways that you can apply these verses:

If then you have been raised with Christ...
When Christ who is your life appears,
then you also will appear with Him in glory.
Put to death therefore what is earthly in you:
sexual immorality, impurity, passion, evil
desire, and covetousness, which is idolatry.
Colossians 3:1-5

3. Find accountability: We have already discussed how important it is to allow others to assist you in your battle and not isolate yourself (Galatians 6:1, Hebrews 3:12-14). Going a step further, it is crucial to invite accountability for specific repentance plans (thought work, the right pursuits, what needs to be put off, and facilitators and inhibitors to sin). Such accountability can come in the form of a meeting with a prayer partner, a pastor or small group leader, a counselor or just a Christian friend that you connect with daily or weekly. Accountability is something that *you* must desire because you want to abide in Christ's love and honor Him (John 15:9; Psalm 40:8). It will not be effective to have others police you against your will while you are resenting it. Accountability must flow out of your own humility and devotion to the Lord. *You* seek it out for the Lord's sake. Then, you will be glad for it and the accountability will be more effective.

> *I have restrained my feet from every evil way,*
> *in order to keep your word.*
> *Psalm 119:101*

4. Develop the personal spiritual disciplines of the Christian life: There are certain means of grace that the Spirit will use to make us more like Christ; serving God and man (2 Peter 3:18). They help us to grow and bless God. Some are: Bible study and meditation, corporate and personal worship, prayer, the Lord's Supper, and ministry to the church body and world (Acts 2:42; Hebrews 10:24-25; 1 Peter 2:2). Each of these will strengthen your faith and your walk with God, making you far less susceptible to your flesh and the schemes of the evil one. One at a time, begin to add them to your life and exercise yourself in them.

Hopefully you can see just how important your own dependent effort is in your Christian walk and especially in mortifying sin. And hopefully you can see the proper motivation for it. Being active in a good church and being accountable can be helpful when beginning or strengthening these new habits.[9] But more than that, you need to rest in the fact that God is going to help you and be the one to grow you. Will you exercise faith in Philippians 1:6?

---

[9] For more on the importance, benefits, and responsibilities of church membership and body life, see Wayne Mack and Dave Swavely, *Life in the Father's House: A Member's Guide to the Local Church* Phillipsburg, NJ: P&R Publishing Co., 2007.

And I am sure of this, that he who began a
good work in you will bring it to
completion at the day of Jesus Christ.
Philippians 1:6

God is patient and very aware that growth in these virtues is a process (Psalm 103:8-14, 2 Corinthians 3:18). He is only asking you to begin with Him and be willing to persevere through the ups and downs. He will be by your side on this journey, will forgive as you confess and repent, and is willing to give everything you need along the way. He is not looking for perfection, but dependent effort—and He will be faithful!

Nevertheless, I am continually with you;
you hold my right hand. You guide me
with your counsel, and afterward you
will receive me to glory.
Psalm 73:23-24

Chapter 7

Radical Love, for Radical Love!

There was a man from my home state of Pennsylvania who knew when to take radical steps for his own good. When Donald Wyman was clearing land in a remote part of the state, a large tree rolled onto his leg, pinning him to the ground. All of his cries for help dissipated into the miles and miles of lonely forest. He eventually concluded that the only way to save his life was to cut off his leg. As traumatic and excruciating as it was, Wyman's amputation of his own leg allowed him to free himself, drive to get help and live.[10]

Our discussions earlier on the need to vivify spiritual exercise begs the questions, "Just how serious do I have to be? How far must I take these things? Do I have to be a fanatic?" This true story illustrates for us the need to do whatever it takes (short of physical amputation, of course) to escape the destructive effects of sin, for our good and God's glory. It should also lead to the question, "Just how trapped am I?" And even more importantly, "Just how far did Christ go for me?" Read about the measure of Christ's love for you and how far He went to make deliverance from sin, its affects and its consequences possible for you.

[Christ] who, though he was in the form of
God, did not count equality with God a thing
to be grasped, but emptied himself, by taking
the form of a servant, being born in the
likeness of men. And being found in human

---

10 Reported in the Minneapolis Star Tribune, July 22, 1993.

form, he humbled himself by becoming
obedient to the point of death,
even death on a cross.
Philippians 2:6-8

He has delivered us from the domain of
darkness and transferred us to the kingdom
of his beloved Son in whom we have
redemption, the forgiveness of sins. He is the
image of the invisible God, the firstborn of
all creation...all things were created through
him and for him. And he is before all things,
and in him all things hold together... And
you, who once were alienated and hostile
In mind, doing evil deeds...he has now
reconciled in his body of flesh by his death,
in order to present you holy and blameless
and above reproach before him...
Colossians 1:13-22

The only response to such a love is radical love itself—an all-out pursuit to please and lay hold of Christ. How can we do anything less than whatever it takes to cut off habitual temptation and sin? The problem is that sin often comes with a certain amount of blindness when it comes to evaluating and implementing appropriate steps. Christ Himself has explained to us just how serious we should be about dealing with our sin.

I encountered one of the most extreme examples of this violation of the no-provision principle when a guy came to me for counsel because he was going to a strip club regularly. He knew it wasn't right and he wanted to stop. I started by asking some questions.

"How often do you do this?"

"Quite often."

"Well, how often?"

"Two to three times a week."

"Where is this place?

"North Hollywood."

"Where is it in relationship to where you live?"

"Well," he said, "I live upstairs in the same building."

He told me that the owner of the building was a friend of the family and she was giving him a really good deal on the rent. As I listened, I was thinking, "What is wrong with this picture?" I let the Word of God speak by referring him to Mathew 5:29: "If your right eye causes you to sin, tear it out and throw it away." This verse means that we must be radical in dealing with temptation and sin, and it does not say you should nurse the eye or be okay with it. No, it says to pluck it out and throw it far from you.

He read the verse and said, "You're not thinking I'm going to have to move from there, are you?" That was exactly what was needed and I told him so. He was not getting the importance of God's command to "make no provision for the flesh." We read the rest of the passage:

*If your right eye causes you to sin, tear it
out and throw it away. For it is better that
you lose one of your members than that your
whole body be thrown into hell.
And if your right hand causes you to sin,
cut it off and throw it away...*
Matthew 5:29-30

We know from other passages where Christ taught, it
is not our eye or our arm that causes us to sin (Mark 7: 20-23).
Christ's point here is to be radical in dealing with habitual sin.
We must be as drastic as we can with it and act with as much
finality as we can. This is how far we are to go. We must be a
zealous warrior for Christ against that which grieves Him and
from that which He died to save us. Purpose to put your sin to
death in the power of Christ because it moves you away from
Him! And when you begin to grow weary, remember this:

*Consider him who endured from sinners
such hostility against himself, so that you
may not grow weary or fainthearted. In your
struggle against sin you have not yet resisted
to the point of shedding your blood [death].*
Hebrews 12:3-4

So, in pursuit of Christ, your best option to mortify your
sin is *radical amputation* of opportunity, *radical appropriation*
of the right priorities and truth, and *radical accountability.* Be
as radical as you possibly can be until there is victory, and stay
as radical as necessary for Christ.

Being radical and watchful in this way means being
quick to abate the flesh or quick to confess and turn away, not
in fear, ever looking for something that might be there. There

is definitely a caution here of not becoming introspective and self-focused. Theologian Martin Lloyd Jones gives us some wise words:

> But what is the difference between examining oneself and becoming introspective? I suggest that we cross the line from self-examination to introspection when, in a sense, we do nothing but examine ourselves, and when such self-examination becomes the main and chief end in our life. We are meant to examine ourselves periodically, but if we are always doing it, always, as it were, putting our soul on a plate and dissecting it, that is introspection. And if we are always talking to people about ourselves and our problems and troubles, and if we are forever going to them with that kind of frown upon our face and saying: I am in great difficulty—it probably means that we are all the time centered upon ourselves. That is introspection, and that in turn leads to the condition known as morbidity."[11]

Being radical means that you will pay attention to and deal with yourself quickly, calling upon God's grace (1 Timothy 4:16; Romans 13:14; Hebrews 4:16). Otherwise, you will miss "the way of escape" which is God providing you with the power to endure all the way through temptation or difficulty (1 Corinthians 10:13).[12] In response to Christ's radical love, there should be a guarding of your heart (true

---

[11] Martin Lloyd-Jones, *Spiritual Depression*, 17.
[12] The phrase "the way of escape" can mean the way to come through and out. In the context of the rest of the verse this is obviously it's meaning here. *The New Linguistic and Exegetical Key to the Greek New Testament*, Gleon L. Rogers Jr. and Gleon L. Rogers III, Grand Rapids, MI, Zondervan Publishing House, 1998, 371).

worship and renewed thoughts) and an alertness to the flesh (selfish desires, thoughts and actions, see Proverbs 4:23; Matthew 26:41). When seeking to mortify sin you should gladly "Be very careful, therefore, to love the LORD YOUR GOD" (Joshua 23:11).

Chapter 8

Will the Real Mortification Please Stand Up?

In our culture today, we see many counterfeits for the real thing; "the real McCoy." There are counterfeit documents, art, money, "knock-off" clothing, watches, and handbags. There are bogus job offers, deceptive people and more. We must be alert and cautious, always on the lookout for what is not genuine. The same could be said for the Christian in his or her daily walk. When sin is not dealt with God's way, it is easy to fall into counterfeits for grace-based and love-based mortification. True mortification is not self-achieved, self-justifying, self-advancing or self-abasing. Such errors are seen in these counterfeits for the real thing:

1. Asceticism (no enjoyments and/or inflicting harm, pain or suffering)
2. Pietism (personal feelings or experience over fact and doctrine),
3. Mysticism (applied to spirituality-supposed communication with God that supersedes Scripture; separating the ministry of the Holy Spirit from God's revealed Word)
4. Quietism theology (will is denied for passivity; "Let go and let God" because He will do it, confusing our position and practice)
5. Antinomianism (any standards, obedience or guards are legalistic, faith without change is sufficient),
6. Legalism (personal works and restraint for a right standing with God, or to maintain His love)

7. Entire Sanctification (living in denial:"I have basically arrived." "I have, or can have, no more sin".)
8. Escaping reality (diversion through business, substance abuse, fanaticizing, recreation)
9. Diverting attention with another sin or crisis (forcing the spotlight or focus elsewhere)

These destructive substitutes only lead to more sin and eventually hopelessness.

Distinguishing Factors that Sin is <u>Not Really</u> Mortified

There are certain distinguishing factors accompanying a sin pattern that has *not* been killed and also a pattern that *has* been. These can also help to determine genuine mortification. Below I have adapted a shorter compilation of what John Owen and Christopher Love have set forth as identifying factors in discerning whether or not a sin is subdued.[13] See where your sin falls in this list and let this identification spur you on to abide in Christ's love and grace, rather than let sin continue unmortified.

1. There is not much distance between you and your sin. It doesn't take a whole lot of effort to choose sin because you have made it so easy. Like the guy who struggles with pornography on his computer, but has not put any guards on it or moved it into the family room, you have not made sin hard and righteousness easier. You foolishly think you can be strong and that there will be no more weak moments. Or you really

---

[13] Christopher Love, *The Mortified Christian*. **"The Mortified Christian"** WARNING - I cannot recommend Love's specific view in this book on page 52. He proof texts Deuteronomy 22:25-27 to teach that a Christian who sins in extreme circumstances cannot be held responsible for his sin, but instead Satan "raped" the believer and therefore Satan is culpable.

aren't ready to give up completely your feeble and destructive means of refuge or pleasure. To use an old puritan adage, your carriage is still parked right outside the door of commission.

2. Very little prayer is prayed against it. It is not on your mind to say, "Lord, help me to say no to that sin." As we learned from Titus 2:11-14, because of God's grace, we must deny ungodliness and worldly desires and live a self-controlled, upright and godly life. But that will not happen if very little prayer is prayed against your sin. If you look back at 1:00 on the Lust Clock, each time temptation comes you are faced with choices. The first is to pray about it or not. Your decision to pray daily about choosing Christ rather than sin reveals how serious you are about mortifying your sin.

3. You commit the sin again with very little temptation. Your heart is like gun powder to sin's touch and the slightest spark triggers ignition. For example, for someone who struggles with pornography the slightest little thing on TV starts full-blown temptation and a wrong choice. Or you see something you want at the mall or are around a compromising person and you are headed quickly back to sin.

4. You take more care in keeping it secret than in seeking help. In pride you wait too long for help or prayer support, setting yourself up for temptation and failure. Your non-aggressive approach to being open with someone who could help you may stem from your desire to keep open your option to sin.

Distinguishing Factors that Sin Is Mortified

1. You Contemplate God's perfections. You will be thinking much more about God's attributes because you will be more focused on Him and the Scriptures. As an act of worship, your goal will be to become more like the example Jesus set for godliness, so that you might please Him above all things, for his glory. (Psalm 27:4-6; 2 Corinthians 5:9)

2. You react strongly toward the first stirring of sin. There are times we cannot stop temptation from knocking at the door of our mind, but we can refuse to let it in by cutting it off. As the phrase goes, when sin is mortified, you will "Nip it! Nip in the bud!" You have learned that if you wait until your heart is around 4 or 5 o'clock on the lust clock, it will be too late. That's like trying to stop a six-ton truck half way down a hill. When sin is mortified you have a new habit of avoiding the slippery slope! (Romans 13:14)

3. You are seeking to live daily dependent on the strength of Christ. You're not trying to live the Christian life on your own because you know you can't. You say, "I need the Lord. I need the help of the Spirit of God through the Word of God. Your prayer is often, "O Lord, hasten to my help!" (Psalm 22:19)

4. You hate all sin, not just one. You find that not only do you hate the old dominating sin in your life, but also you begin to see and hate all sin because it moves you away from Christ. You love and pursuing holiness because you see the beauty of the Lord and His way to live. (Psalm 27:4; Psalm 40:8)

5. Your goal is all about Christ, not self. If your focus is on Christ, rather than self, then real mortification is taking place. Selfish goals are apparent when your priority is the approval of other people, or your heart's desire is to be esteemed, to have a better life, or to feel better about yourself. If your purpose for pursuing holiness flows out of gratitude and a desire for an abiding walk with Christ, for his Honor and glory, then you are engaged in God's kind of mortification. (John 15:1-11; 2 Corinthians 5:9; Romans 13:14a)

To sum up all that has been discussed thus far, here is a practical definition of mortification:

> A discipline of grace whereby a Christian pursues holiness for the surpassing value of Christ, by exercising faith and the practical means of grace God has given to **aggressively** but **dependently** strive against a particular habitual sin (the triumph of the flesh), thus weakening its grip and subduing its dominance until it is *practically* dead.[14]

---

[14] The word "mortify" literally means "to put to death". (Linguistic Key, page 330.)

Chapter 9

Where the Rubber Meets the Road

It wouldn't do much good to run a foot race with a 20 pound sack of potatoes on your back! Likewise, to realize a true pursuit of Christ and victory over sin, it is important to consider some personal hindrances and practical applications concerning your own particular sin struggle. All of these are either related to manifestations of pride, or lack of true devotion and humility. There are many more; this is not an exhaustive list. Read through the list below and respond with the appropriate confessions, prayers, commitments and action plans necessary for actually following through on all you have learned. Take your time, making your faith and hope active in a practical way!

Personal Hindrances to a Grace Pursuit

1. You are not saved. This is, of course, *the ultimate* hindrance. We don't stand a chance for lasting change from the inside out if we are outside of Christ. If you are an unbeliever, you are still under the law of sin (its power) and you love to sin. Some people think they are saved and they are not. As Second Corinthians 13:5 encourages us, it is a good thing to examine your faith with the Scriptures because the natural or unsaved person cannot be transformed.

> *The natural person does not accept the things of the spirit of God, for they are folly to him, and he is not able to understand them because they are spiritually discerned.*
> *1 Corinthians 2:14*

2. Laziness. Nothing puts a kink in the best laid plans as much as laziness. Some people quit because they find they can't coast into godliness. We must exercise ourselves unto godliness, and that takes dependent work.

> *Now for this very reason also,*
> *applying all diligence, in your faith supply*
> *moral excellence, and in your moral*
> *excellence, knowledge.*
> *2 Peter 1:5, NASB*

3. Apathy. Giving up or not taking things seriously will only lead to greater sin and disaster. Some people just don't care. Sometimes the sin cycle goes on for so long, a person just gets tired of it, becomes apathetic, and thinks, *"Why try? I've never defeated this thing before. It is just the way it is."* It hasn't worked because you haven't taken seriously the resources God has given you.

> *Do not be slothful in zeal, be*
> *fervent in spirit, serve the Lord.*
> *Romans 12:11*

4. Treasuring Secret Sin. When we treasure a secret sin, we want to keep our sin quiet and not tell anyone about our problem. We start to believe that if we don't tell anyone, then it's not a big problem. When we treasure secret sin, it means we are not treasuring Christ and hating sin the way He does. This is a serious matter because according to Psalm 66:18, it is also a hindrance to our communion with God. Thankfully, we also have Psalm 32:3-5:

> *When I kept silent about my sin, my body*
> *wasted away through my groaning all day*
> *long. For day and night Your hand was*

> *heavy upon me; my vitality was drained*
> *away as with the fever heat of summer. I*
> *acknowledged my sin to You, and my iniquity*
> *I did not hide; I said, "I will confess my*
> *transgressions to the LORD"; and You*
> *forgave the guilt of my sin.*
> *NASB*

5. Weariness. Sometimes we *do* become weary in well doing; especially if we are going along in our own strength. In Galatians; 6:7-9 there is a warning and a promise. Keep persevering in your spiritual walk with Christ; rather than giving in to the feelings of weariness that can accompany dealing with sin in your life. Call on God to strengthen and refresh you in His Word. He knows when and how to bring relief and blessing. And of course, full rest will be waiting for us in heaven!

> *God is not mocked. Whatever a man sows*
> *that will he reap and Let us not lose heart in*
> *doing good, for in due time we will reap if we*
> *do not grow weary.*
> *Galatians 6:7-9*

6. Ignorance of Theology. I remember that in the first four years of my Christian life, I was not growing much in my faith because I was "letting go and letting God." I adopted a false theology of sanctification, praying, "Oh Lord, please take the lust away, please take the problems away, please take the difficult people out of my life." That was my letting go. What I was actually expecting was for God to obey me. And yet, He commands *us* to deal with lust, problems, and difficult people in the ways He has told us, with the help of the Holy Spirit, and I wasn't doing a thing! It was a kind of stalemate and I wasn't growing much. It is important to be in the Word and personally to adopt biblical theology about sin, sanctification, and the Christian life.

See to it that no one takes you captive
by philosophy and empty deceit, according
to human tradition, according to the
elemental spirits of the world,
and not according to Christ.
Colossians 2:8

7. Misplaced Priorities. Let's face it. We are prone to distraction. Our priorities are misplaced when we are giving our greatest attention to temporary things of this world, rather than to Christ and pleasing Him. Then we will be stunted in our growth in the faith. This can even include getting so busy *doing* ministry that we give little thought about our daily relationship with Christ and *being* who God wants us to be.

If then you have been raised with Christ,
seek the things that are above . . . set your
mind on things that are above, not on things
that are on earth . . . When Christ who is
your life appears, then you will appear with
him in glory. Put to death therefore
what is also earthly in you.
Colossians 3:1-5

8. Bad Company. The verse, *"bad company ruins good morals"* begins with *"Do not be deceived . . ." (1 Corinthians 15:33)*. So don't ever be deceived, thinking that friendship with non-Christians doesn't matter. Purpose to find friends who seek God's will in their lives and are eager to bring glory to Him. No matter how resolved you are in your faith, hanging out with people who indulge in sinful habits will take you down! Watch out for this pitfall.

Suggested Personal Applications

- Slow down to meditate on Christ and the Gospel of Christ every day. Consider what Christ did on your behalf and what your union with Him means to your identity and your Christian walk. (Luke 7:47)

> *Indeed, I count everything as loss because*
> *of the surpassing worth of knowing Christ*
> *Jesus my Lord. For his sake I have suffered*
> *the loss of all things and count them as*
> *rubbish, in order that I may gain Christ.*
> *Philippians 3:8*

- View the sin you are dealing with as worshiping something other than Christ and your choice to sin as forsaking Christ's love and choosing rubbish or broken cisterns. Write down any idols or false refuges you may have. Confess them and pray about forsaking them daily. (1 John 5:21)

> *. . . for my people have committed two evils:*
> *they have forsaken me, the fountain of living waters,*
> *and hewed out cisterns for themselves,*
> *broken cisterns that can hold no water.*
> *Jeremiah 2:13*

- Create a "thankful" list about Christ, His realities and blessings. (Colossians 4:2)

> *Let the word of Christ dwell in you richly,*
> *teaching and admonishing one another in*
> *all wisdom, singing psalms and hymns and*
> *spiritual songs, with thankfulness*
> *in your hearts to God.*
> *Colossians 3:16*

- Focus on pursuing, knowing and putting on the Lord Jesus Christ each day and in all your efforts. Devote time each day to meeting with God through the Word and prayer and seek to continue through your day in dependence and worship (Philippians 3: 10-11; 1Thessalonians 5:17; Romans 13:14; Revelation 2:5)

> *But put on the Lord Jesus Christ,*
> *and make no provision for the flesh,*
> *to gratify its desires.*
> *Romans 13:14*

- Be watchful about doubt, discouragement or fear so you can outline when and why you need to exercise your faith. Write these realizations down with Scripture to keep on hand (Habakkuk 2:4; Hebrews 10:23; 1 Peter 5:8-9)

> *But now that you have come to know God,*
> *or rather to be known by God, how can you*
> *turn back again to the weak and worthless*
> *elementary principles of the world, whose*
> *slaves you want to be once more?*
> *Galatians 4:9*

- Practice repentance *with faith* as a lifestyle. Write on a card what you need to have faith in when you confess your sin. (Isaiah 55:7; Romans 15:13)

> *. . . and since we have a great priest over*
> *the house of God, let us draw near with a*
> *true heart in full assurance of faith, with*
> *our hearts sprinkled clean from an evil*
> *conscience and our bodies washed with*
> *pure water. Let us hold fast the confession*

of our hope without wavering,
for he who promised is faithful.
Hebrews 10:21-23

- Contemplate each day Christ's return and spending eternity with Him. (1 John 3:2-3; Romans 8: 18-25; 1 Corinthians 15:50-58)

> *Then I saw a new heaven and a new earth,*
> *for the first heaven and the first earth had*
> *passed away, and the sea was no more. ² And*
> *I saw the holy city, new Jerusalem, coming*
> *down out of heaven from God, prepared as*
> *a bride adorned for her husband. ³ And I*
> *heard a loud voice from the throne saying,*
> *"Behold, the dwelling place of God is with*
> *man. He will dwell with them, and they will*
> *be his people, and God himself will be with*
> *them as their God. ⁴ He will wipe away every*
> *tear from their eyes, and death shall be no*
> *more, neither shall there be mourning, nor*
> *crying, nor pain anymore, for the former*
> *things have passed away."*
> *Revelation 21:1-4*

- Outline what the righteous alternatives to your sins are, and begin pursuing them with zeal. Write down what they are (with Scripture) and practical ways you can pursue them. (Colossians 3:5-16)

> *. . . assuming that you have heard about him*
> *and were taught in him, as the truth is in*
> *Jesus, to put off your old self, which belongs*
> *to your former manner of life and is corrupt*
> *through deceitful desires, and to be renewed*

> *in the spirit of your minds, and to put on the*
> *new self, created after the likeness of God in*
> *true righteousness and holiness.*
> *Ephesians 4:21-24*

- Outline hindrances to temptation and sin so that you can employ them and no provision (opportunity) is made for the lust of your flesh. Make concrete plans to follow through.

> *But put on the Lord Jesus Christ,*
> *and make no provision for the flesh,*
> *to gratify its desires.*
> *Romans 13:14*

- Outline facilitators to temptation and sin so you can cut them off (amputate) radically. Make concrete plans to follow through.

> *If your right eye causes you to sin, tear it*
> *out and throw it away. For it is better that*
> *you lose one of your members than that your*
> *whole body be thrown into hell. And if*
> *your right hand causes you to sin,*
> *cut it off and throw it away. For it is*
> *better that you lose one of your members*
> *than that your whole body go into hell.*
> *Matthew 5:29-30*

- Watch for, write down and correct wrong thoughts (discouragements, rationalizations and lies) associated with your sin habit, by renewing them with God's truth and promises. Record these new thoughts that are full of thankfulness, truth and faith on index cards. Concretely repent of your thinking in this way.

> *Do not be conformed to this world, but be*
> *transformed by the renewal of your mind,*
> *that by testing you may discern what is*
> *the will of God, what is good and*
> *acceptable and perfect.*
> **Romans 12:2**

- Determine specifically how you will start minimizing times of isolation and eliminating bad company by seeking out good Christian friendships, communicating your struggle and enlisting help. (Hebrews 10:24-25; Galatians 6:1)

> *Whoever isolates himself seeks his own desire;*
> *he breaks out against all sound judgment.*
> **Proverbs 18:1**

- Determine exactly where you need to be held accountable and seek out a specific accountability partner. (Hebrews 3:12-14)

> *I hold back my feet from every evil way,*
> *in order to keep your word.*
> **Psalm 119:101**

- Write down new ways you can pursue loving and serving God in various places and activities in which you are engaged (Romans 12:10-11; Psalm 100:2).

> *Love one another with brotherly affection.*
> *Outdo one another in showing honor.*
> *Do not be slothful in zeal, be fervent in*
> *spirit, serve the Lord.*
> **Psalm 110:2**

- Write down the personal spiritual disciplines mentioned in this book. Determine and record how you are going to add them to your life in light of the Gospel. (1 Timothy 4:10)

> *Have nothing to do with irreverent, silly myths. Rather train yourself for godliness; for while bodily training is of some value, godliness is of value in every way, as it holds promise for the present life and also for the life to come. The saying is trustworthy and deserving of full acceptance.*
> *1 Timothy 4:7-9*

- Ask yourself if you are being radical (diligent and fervent in spirit) in carrying out all these practical ways to mortify your sin (Romans 12:11; Joshua 23:11; Matthew 5:29-30).

> *For the grace of God has appeared, bringing salvation for all people, training us to renounce ungodliness and worldly passions, and to live self-controlled, upright, and godly lives in the present age, waiting for our blessed hope, the appearing of the glory of our great God and Savior Jesus Christ, who gave himself for us to redeem us from all lawlessness and to purify for himself a people for his own possession who are zealous for good works.*
> *Titus 2:11-14*

- Create a prayer list of things you need to pray about given what you have learned, including ways that others can pray for you. Pray without ceasing! (Ephesians 6:18; 1 Thessalonians 5:17).

> *... praying at all times in the Spirit, with all prayer and supplication. To that end keep alert with all perseverance, making supplication for all the saints ...*
> *Ephesians 6:18*

Chapter 10

Final Thoughts

Take heart, friend. You are not the proverbial exception! You *can* by the Gospel and by biblical principles of change that God has given us put off sin, walk with Christ as He intended and be useful in His kingdom! Indeed, you *must*. Do not believe the great deceptions of the evil one, who wants you to believe, "God is not good or sufficient," "I can never change," "It is not worth it," or "What would God want with me?" You have a Savior who has demonstrated the depth of His love and that is all you need. And you are not alone. Many have gone before you and found victory. It is time to appropriate all that the Christ of surpassing value has for you. Cry out to God in repentance with faith, ask for the Spirit's help and get going!

Seek out others with the same passion for Christ and against sin. My prayer for you as you seek to apply the truth you have read to your life and heart is the same as Paul's prayer for the Corinthian believers when he encouraged them with the sure hope that they will be changed in a moment, in the twinkling of eye, at the last trumpet:

> *Therefore, my beloved brothers, be steadfast,*
> *immovable, always abounding in the work of*
> *the Lord, knowing that in the Lord*
> *your labor is not in vain.*
> *1 Corinthians 15:58*

We began this book with thoughts by the great John Owen, and so it is fitting that we close with a quote by him that is probably the most important thing to remember on the topic of mortifying our sin.

> Mortification can never be thought of as separated from the ministry of the Holy Spirit. He brings the work to a consummation. He convinces of sin in the first place, and reveals the help that is in Christ. He establishes the heart to expect relief, and He alone brings the cross of Christ into our hearts with its sin-killing power; for by the Spirit we are baptized into the death of Christ. He is both Author and Finisher of sanctification. His presence gives support in this essential work.[15]

Other Quotes by Puritan Brethren

- "True mourning for sin must flow from spiritual convictions of the evil, and vileness, and dimmable nature of sin . . . true mourning for sin is more for the evil that is in sin, than the evil that comes by sin; more because it dishonors God, and wounds Christ, and grieves the Spirit, and makes the soul unlike God, than because it damns the soul. Now, there are many that mourn for sin, not so much for the evil that is in it, as for the evil that it brings with it. . . ." (Matthew Mead, *The Almost Christian Discovered*, 56-57).

- "A truly mortified man is like a warrior: he will either kill or be killed. He will kill his sins or else his sin will kill him. Now examine yourselves in this: are you only fencers, to sport and play with your lusts, or are you warriors who fight with an implacable opposition against sin? Do you only give a slight scare to sin or have you given it a deadly wound?" (Christopher Love, *The Mortified Christian*, 38).

---

[15] John Owen, Sin and Temptation, 86

- "... sin always seeks to extenuate and lessen the seriousness of sin to the mind. 'It is only a small offense,' it says. 'It will be given up shortly.' With such excuses it speaks the language of a deceived heart. When there is a readiness on the part of the soul to listen to these silent voices—secret insinuations that arise from deceit—it is evident that the affections are already enticed. When the soul willingly listens to these seductions, it has already lost its affections for Christ, and has become seduced. Sin entices like 'wine when it is red, when it gives its color in the cup, when it moves itself attractively' (Proverbs 23:31). But in the end, sin 'bites like a serpent, and stings like an adder'" (23:32). (John Owen, 60).

- "Though Christ justifies us from the guilt of sin, we must labor [with Him] to be freed from the filth of sin." (Christopher Love, 4, *addition mine)*.

- "Mortification prunes all the graces of God, and makes room for them in our hearts to grow." (John Owen, Mortification of Sin, 352).

- "Exercise and success (in mortification) are the two main cherishers of grace in the heart, let not that man think he makes any progress in holiness who walks not over the bellies of his lusts." (John Owen, 15).

- "Fill your affections with the cross of Christ and you will find no room for sin." (John Owen, 62).

- "Set faith at work on Christ for the killing of thy sin . . . . Live in this, and thou wilt die a conqueror . . ." (John Owen, 291).

- "Many do their sins as mariners do by their goods, cast them out in a storm, wishing for them again in a calm . . . Many confess their sins, but with no intent to forsake sin; they confess the sins they have committed, but do not leave the sins they have confessed." (Mead, 59).

- "Exercise grace whenever you would see it; idle habits are not perceived. Believe and repent till you feel that you do believe and repent, and love God till you feel that you love Him." (Richard Baxter, *Christian Directory*, 903).

Battle Plan for Killing Sin Habits

Always be **P.R.E.P.A.R.E.D.** for Spiritual Battle by
Continually Abiding in Christ

1. <u>P</u>RAY

A. Adoration

C. Confession

T. Thanksgiving

S. Supplication (for self and others)

Submit my will to God's (Luke 22:42) and seek to please Him (2 Corinthians 5:9).

2. <u>R</u>EHEARSE Gospel Truths (New Man in Christ—position to practice) and God's attributes, deeds and promises as well as His love for me in Christ.

A. What Jesus did in His life, death and resurrection out of love for me

B. What Repentance and Faith mean and look like in my life

C. Who I am as a New Man in Christ (Galatians 5:24, old man crucified, and now I'm alive in Christ)

D. How I should live as His Adopted Child out of love for Him in holiness

E. Who is God (various attributes, Sovereign, Good, Merciful, Just, etc)

F. What has God done (His mighty deeds...)

G. What are His promises (Future grace and Hope)

Faith: "is the life-dominating conviction *and practice* that all God has for me through obedience *to His revealed Word* is better by far than anything Satan can offer me through my selfishness and sin." *The Obedience Factor*, D. Hegg, 28 adapted by Stuart Scott.

3. **E**VALUATE and set my heart to exercise my God-given faith for God's Glory (2 Corinthians 3:18; 2 Peter 3:18).

A. My Thoughts

1. Gird up my Mind on Jesus (1 Peter 1:13; 5:8).
2. Set Mind on the Eternal (Matthew 6:33; Colossians 3:1-4).
3. Take every thought Captive (2 Corinthians 10:5; Philippians 4:8).
4. Deal with my selfish "I deserve and I need" thinking of self-pity and replace them with thankful and contented thoughts about Jesus (Philippians 4:6-9).
5. Who am I to love at this moment? God and others, not me (Matthew 22:37-39).
6. Actively worship and serve God and minister to others day and night (Luke 17:7-10).

B. My Affections

1. To please Christ who gave Himself for me (Titus 2:11-14) for the glory of God (1 Corinthians 10:31) as one who will give an account (2 Corinthians 5:9-10).
2. Be aware of and mortify my specific lusts (Romans 8:13; 13:14).
3. My pursuit of comfort and ease (when not at work).
4. My pursuit of fleshly pleasures (rationalizing and giving in to eating, spending, TV, etc.).
5. My pursuit of escape from God-given pressures

and seeking false refuges.

C. My Choices

1. Because I'm a new creature in Christ and called to holiness and self-control: "By God's grace I will not . . . and I will . . . ." (Psalm 101; Titus 2:11-14).

2. Say No: Buffet my body and mortify my flesh (1 Corinthians 9:27; Romans 8:13).

3. Say Yes: Put on the Lord Jesus (Romans 13:14).

4. How am I going to love and serve Jesus and others right now (be specific and concrete)? (Matthew 22:37-39).

4. **PUT OFF old and PUT ON Jesus** (the whole Armor of God, keep Meditating on God's Word (Romans 13:14; Ephesians 6:10-20; Joshua 1:8; Jeremiah 2:13). Jesus (God's Grace) is teaching me Titus 2:11-14 (cf. 1 Thessalonians 4:1-8):

> **"For the grace of God has appeared, bringing salvation for all people, training us to renounce ungodliness and worldly passions, and to live self-controlled, upright, and godly lives in the present age, waiting for our blessed hope, the appearing of the glory our great God and savior Jesus Christ, who gave himself for us to redeem us from all lawlessness and to purify for himself a people for his own possession who are zealous for good works"** (emphasis mine).

5. **ACTION** (Implement "Charge ahead" with my thoughts, affections and decisions)

A. Obey and Do the Word out of Love for Jesus (James 1:22ff; John 14:21-23).

    B. What's my specific plan and what are my concrete steps? RIGHT NOW!! (with no delay "nip it in the bud").

    C. Remove any provision for the flesh—right away (Romans 13:14).

    D. Remember: The Blessing of God comes in the doing (John 13:17; James 1:25).

6. **RELOAD** with God's Word—keep it up (never a cease fire and never a single-shot battle) (Luke 4:1-13; Psalm 119:9-11). All the resources are there for life and godliness (2 Peter 1:3ff).

7. **ENLIST** others to Help and Pray (Romans 15:30).

    A. Throw out the welcome mat for others to help me and be honest with them (Galatians 6:1ff; Ephesians 4:25).

    B. Pursue fellowship with other godly brothers and couples (Hebrews 10:24-25).

8. **DEPENDENT** on the Holy Spirit for help (in prayer and on His Word) (Zechariah 4:6; Romans 8:13; Galatians 5:16-17; Ephesians 6:18; Philippians 2:13).

> **"Therefore, since we are surrounded by so great a cloud of witnesses, let us also lay aside every weight, and sin which clings so closely, and let us run with endurance the race that is set before us, looking to Jesus, the founder and perfecter of our faith, who for the joy that was set before him endured the cross, despising the shame, and is seated at the right hand of the throne of God."**
>
> **Hebrews 12:1-2**

Resources

Ferguson, Sinclair B, *John Owen on the Christian Life,* Banner of Truth, Horsham, PA, 1987.

Hodges, Brian G., *Licensed to Kill: A Field Manual for Mortifying Sin,* Cruciform Press, 2011.

Love, Christopher, *The Mortified Christian,* Soli Deo Gloria Ministries, 2003.

Lundgaard, Kris, *The Enemy Within,* P & R Publishing Co, 1998.

Mack, Wayne and Mack, Joshua, A *Fight to the Death,* P & R Publishing Co, 2006.

Mead, Matthew, *The Almost Christian Discovered,* Kessinger Publishing, 2007.

Owen, John, *Overcoming Sin and Temptation,* Crossway Publishers, 2006
.
Rogers, Cleon L. Jr., and Rogers, Cleon L. III, *The New Linguistic and Exegetical key to the Greek New Testament,* Zondervan Publishing House, 1998.

Venning, Ralph, *The Sinfulness of Sink,* Banner of Truth, 1996.

Watson, Thomas, *The Doctrine of Repentance,* Banner of Truth.

Our Website: www.oneeightycounseling.com

More Books by Stuart Scott

The Exemplary Husband: A Biblical Perspective
   Study Guide
   Leader's Guide

Biblical Manhood

Booklets: From Pride to Humility
     Communication and Conflict Resolution
     Anger, Anxiety and Fear